Investigate the natural and human features of Australia as you practise your Victorian Modern Cursive script.

My name is

My teacher's name is

My school is

My favourite place in Australia is

Learning goal: To improve knowledge of the alphabet in Victorian Modern Cursive script

Success criteria:

- I can trace and write all lower-case and capital letters of the alphabet in Victorian Modern Cursive.
- I can trace and write all lower-case and capital letters of the alphabet in Victorian Modern Cursive using appropriate size, spacing and slope.

Are you ready to write?

Posture

Ensure your feet are flat on the floor and you are sitting well back in the chair.

Paper position

left-handed

Hold the paper with your non-writing hand.

right-handed

Pencil grip

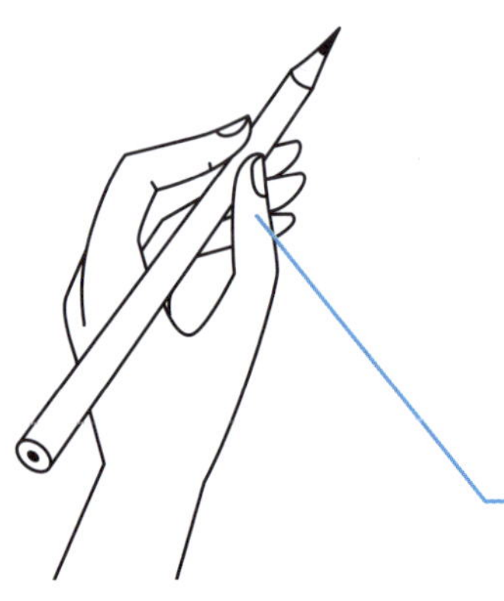

left-handed

Hold your pen or pencil with one finger on top of the barrel.

Support the barrel with your thumb.

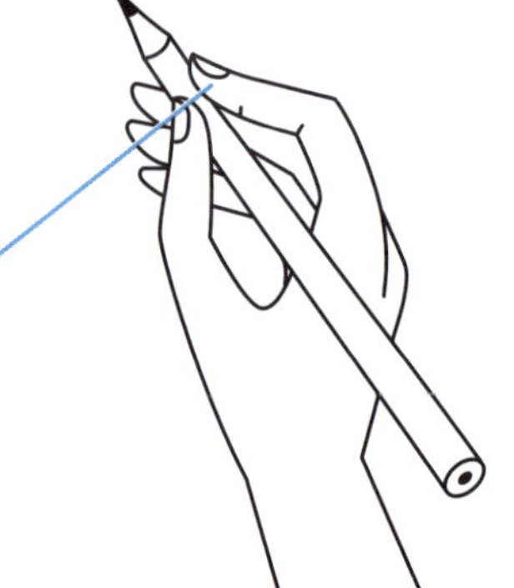

right-handed

Correct letter formation

Trace and copy the lower-case letters. Then circle the letters that spell the word 'geography'.

a b c d e f g h i j k l m

n o p q r s t u v w x y z

Trace and copy the capital letters.

ISBN: 9780170424066

Trace around the maps of Australia and write the letters under the correct headings.

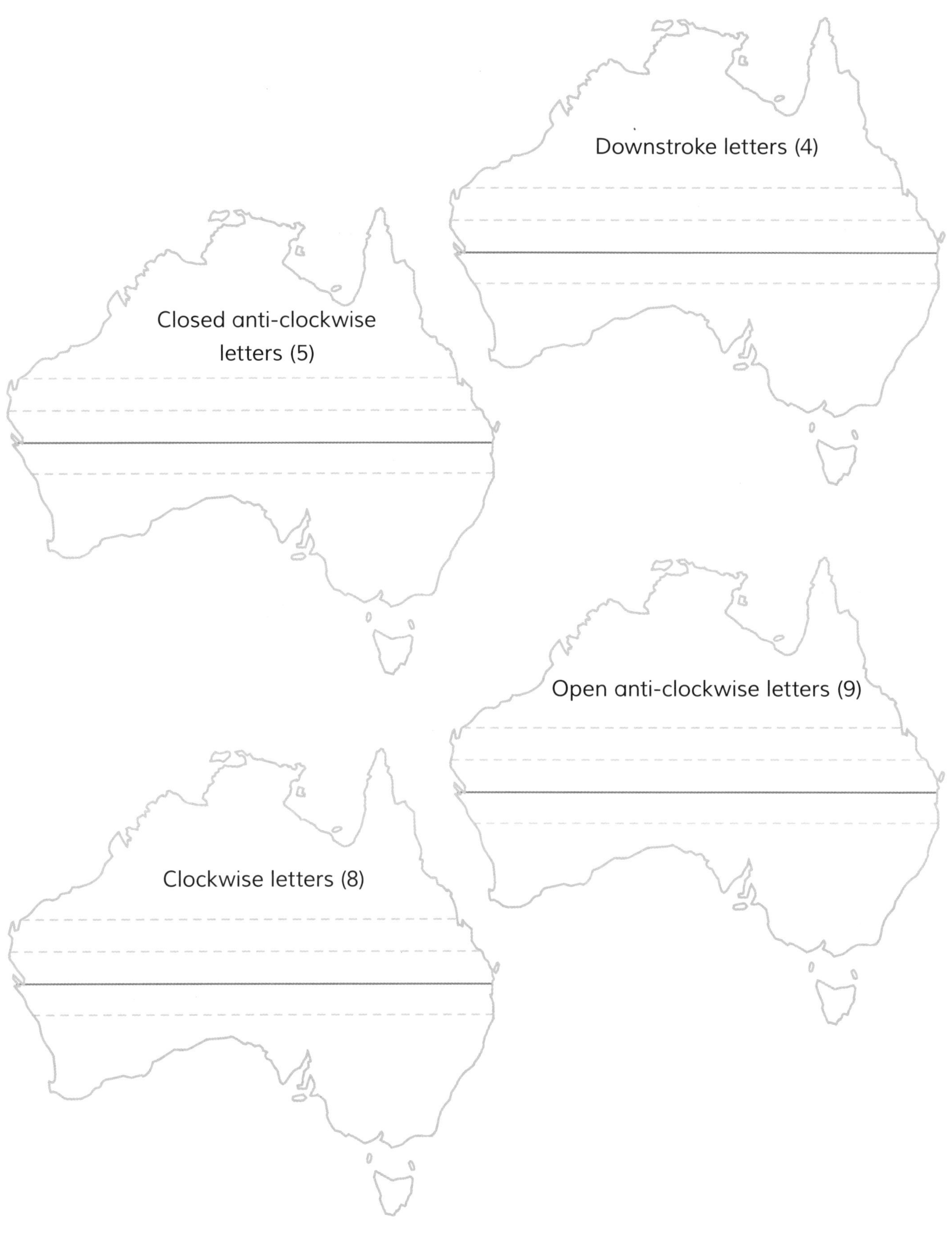

a b c d e f g h i j k l m n o p q r s t u v w x y z

Copy the place names in lower-case letters, then in capital letters.

Victoria VICTORIA

Kooyong KOOYONG

Euroa EUROA

Mildura MILDURA

Warragul WARRAGUL

Self-assessment

Rate your lower-case and capital letters.

☐	☐	☐
I need more practice.	They are improving.	My letters look great!

ISBN: 9780170424066

Diagonal joins

Diagonal joins meet the next letter at the magic line. Extend the exit flick of the first letter to join to the second letter.

Trace and copy these letter pairs and words with diagonal joins.

ap dj ev pi ty di au pu

am ci eu hi ke lu im xi

xy te ue an cu ei nu hu

live Uluru upper never

happen evening didgeridoo

A diagonal join from 'q' can be tricky. You need to change direction quickly and go all the way to the top of the magic line.

Once you practise, it is easy because the movement is the same every time – a 'q' is always followed by a 'u'.

Trace and copy.

qu qu qu qu qu qu qu qu

question quoll quokka

Copy.

Clever geography students ask questions about the habitats of quolls and quokkas.

Diagonal joins to ascenders

al → al

Remember: diagonal joins to ascenders meet at the magic line.

Sweep up and retrace part of the ascender.

Trace and copy these letter pairs with diagonal joins to ascenders.

ab al at cl ch ck el eb et

ll mb ml nt nh th tt ul ub

Trace and copy these words with diagonal joins to ascenders.

clever their about culture

dwell country rock spatial

call change special sunset

Remember: when making a diagonal join to 'f', continue the exit of the letter before and form a loop. The crossbar is a separate stroke.

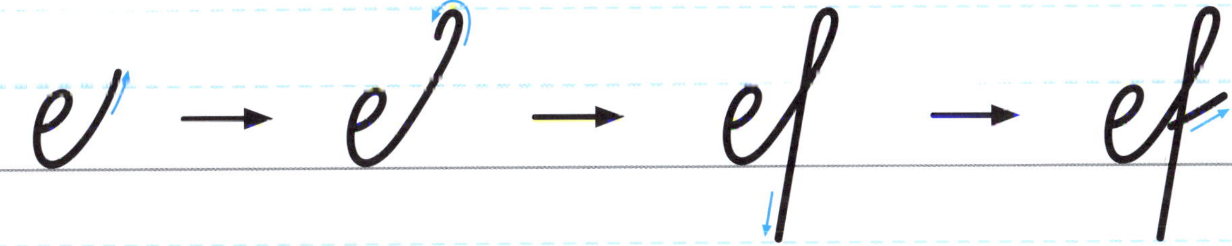

Trace and copy.

af ef if uf lf af ef if uf lf

Remember: don't use a loop when 'f' is at the start of a word.

Trace and copy.

flight wolf effort formation

difference shelf famous lift

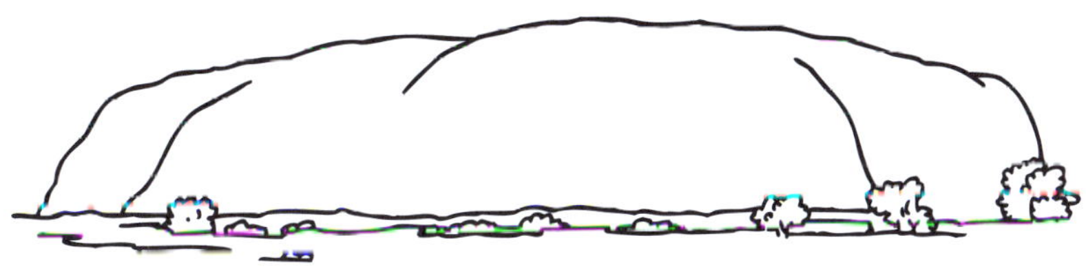

ISBN: 9780170424066

Self-assessment: Diagonal joins

Copy the text. Remember to be careful with your diagonal joins.

The Anangu Aboriginal
people have requested that
visitors don't climb Uluru, as
it is a sacred place. This also
keeps the rock safe from erosion.

Self-assessment

Rate your diagonal joins.

☐ I need practice.

☐ They are improving.

☐ My diagonal joins are great!

get.ga/PMWA170

ISBN: 9780170424066

Touch joins

a c d g q

pen lift

ma

Diagonal joins to the anti-clockwise letters above can be tricky, so we use touch joins. Remember: when joining to one of these letters, make a long exit, then lift your pen and drop in the second letter.

Trace.

a c d g q a c d g q

Trace and copy these letter pairs with touch joins.

ac ca id ug uq ic ua ud

ag aq ma uc ad ig eq cc

Use two colours to copy these words with touch joins.

great sea marine algae

Copy these words with touch joins. The blue dots show which joins are touch joins.

island creatures endangered

places camouflage predator

Add a dot above every touch join in the text below. Then copy the text.

The Great Barrier Reef is one of the Seven Wonders of the World and must be managed carefully for the future.

Self-assessment: Touch joins

Copy the text. Remember to be careful with your touch joins.

People who live in Australia

enjoy many aquatic sports

like surfing and canoeing.

After these activities, it is

refreshing to eat an icy pole.

Self-assessment

Rate your touch joins.

☐ I need practice.

☐ They are getting better.

☐ My touch joins are excellent!

Horizontal joins

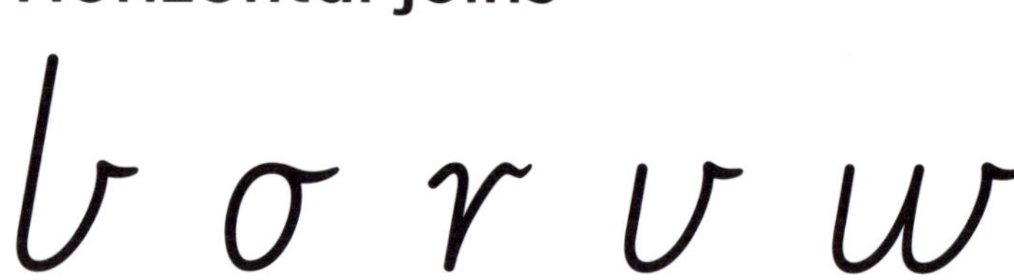

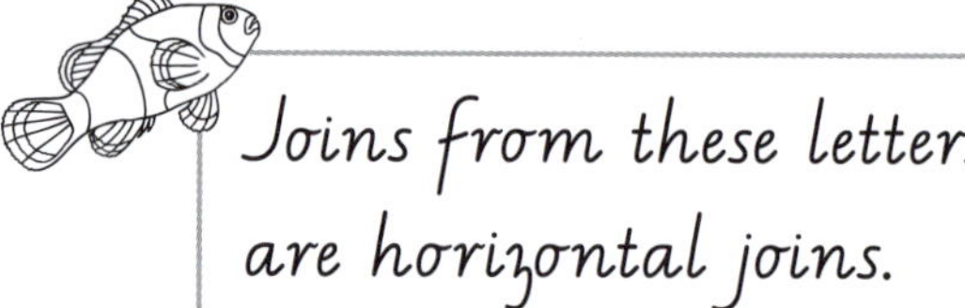

Joins from these letters are horizontal joins.

magic line ba

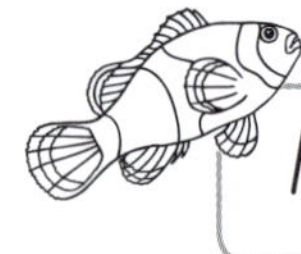

Horizontal joins meet the next letter at the magic line.

Trace and copy these letter pairs with horizontal joins.

or rn wr ox rr ba bi by

wn om wm on rn br bu

wu op ri vy wi ov ru vi

Copy these words with horizontal joins.

enjoy frown wrong corals

bright variety protect swim

Horizontal joins to anti-clockwise letters

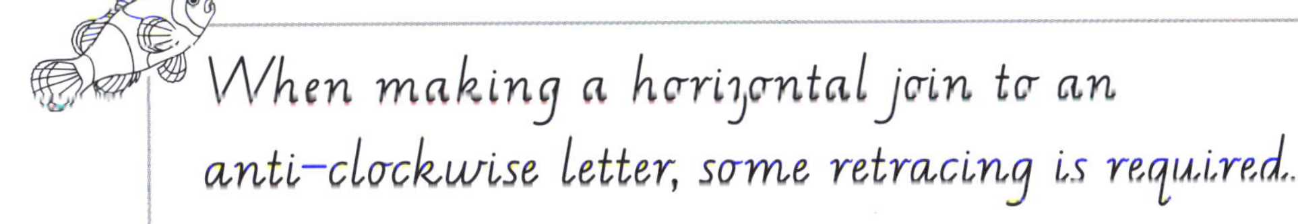

Trace and copy these letter pairs and words with horizontal joins to anti-clockwise letters.

ro ra wa ra va ro ra wa ra

rainfall vary water coral

oo ro vo oa rd oo ro vo oa

codfish ocean evolve road

od og rc od og rc od og rc

ISBN: 9780170424066

Horizontal joins to ascenders

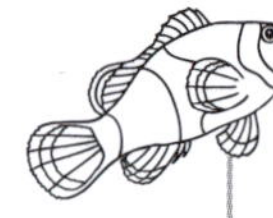

Remember: when joining horizontally to an ascender, sweep up and retrace a little.

rfa

Remember: when making a horizontal join to 'f', continue the exit of the letter before and form a loop. Use the crossbar to join to the next letter.

Make your own letter pairs with horizontal joins to ascenders.

b o r v w to b f h k l t

ob

Trace and copy these words. Underline each horizontal join to an ascender.

world polyps white throttle

pearl colours whistle whales

Trace and copy these words with horizontal joins to 'f'.

surf soft surface overfishing

ISBN: 9780170424066

Self-assessment: Horizontal joins

Copy the text. Remember to be careful with your horizontal joins.

Swimming and snorkelling
at the Great Barrier Reef can
be so much fun. You may
see colourful fish and coral,
turtles, or even a whale.

get.ga/PMWA171

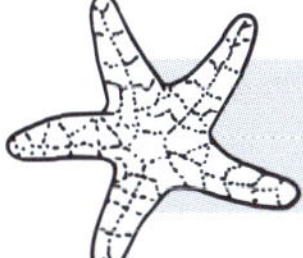

Self-assessment

Rate your horizontal joins.

☐ I need practice.

☐ I'm getting better.

☐ My horizontal joins are excellent!

ISBN: 9780170424066

Clockwise finishers g, j, y and z

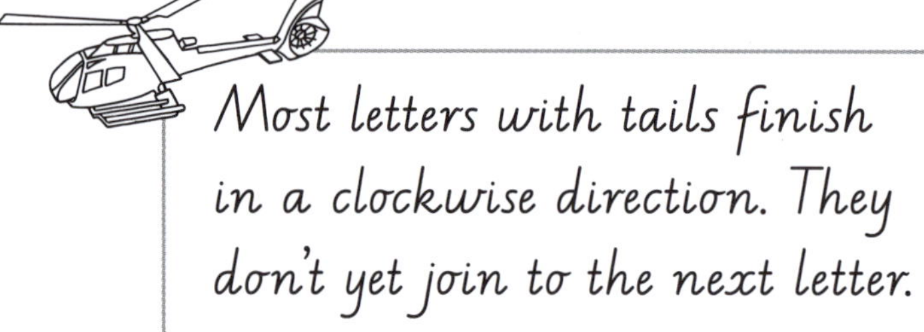

Find, trace and copy only the four letters below that do not join to the next letter.

c d z y i g s j u q

Put a blue dot where there will be no join in cursive.

great	bridge	geography	project
flight	jutting	yacht	amazing
jagged	photograph	ozone	majestic

Prove your answers by writing the words in cursive.

Write the plural forms of the words below by adding 's'. Place a tick above the letters that are clockwise finishers in each word. Did you remember to leave them unjoined?

layer light change

seagull pathway gem

Copy the text and underline the non-joining letter pairs.

The sight of the Twelve
Apostles is just breathtaking.
Flying over them gives an
amazing view from above.

ISBN: 9 780170424066

Self-assessment: Clockwise finishers g, j, y and z

Rewrite the text in cursive. Remember to be careful with letters with descenders.

Victoria's Twelve Apostles are

found along the Great Ocean

Road. These layered limestone

stacks were formed by the

ongoing erosion of high cliffs.

Self-assessment

Rate your use of clockwise finishers.

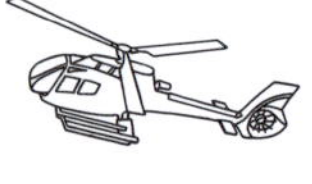

☐ I'm just getting started.

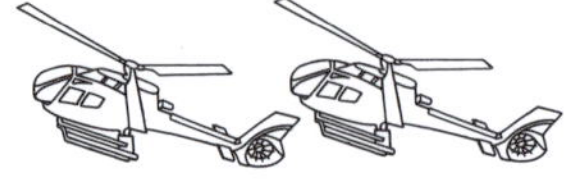

☐ I'm taking off.

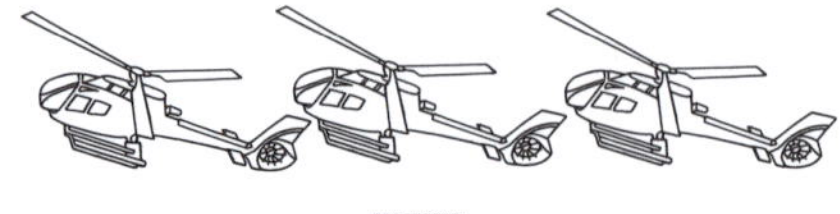

☐ I'm flying high!

Using smaller lines

Smaller writing lines help you to write more quickly. Try to keep your letters a consistent size. It will make your writing legible, or easy to read.

Practise using smaller writing lines. Copy the text.

The Naracoorte Caves are located in South Australia. They are part of a World Heritage site. There are many large caves at Naracoorte that have acted as animal traps for over 500 000 years. The fossils inside are of great interest to palaeontologists.

ISBN: 9780170424066

Self-assessment: Using smaller lines

Copy the text. Take care to write legibly in the smaller lines.

The Blanche Cave was the first cave in
the Naracoorte region to be discovered.
It was once used by the local people as
a community space. They would have
picnics inside the cave on hot days to
escape the summer heat. Now, the only
residents are a colony of bats.

Self-assessment

Rate how legible your handwriting is in smaller lines.

☐ I can improve.

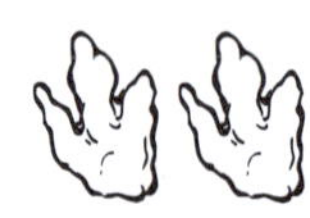

☐ I'm getting there.

☐ I'm doing well!

ISBN: 9780170424066

Spacing

Maintaining even spacing between letters and words helps to keep your handwriting easy to read.

✗ wild life

Rewrite each line of text with even spacing between letters and words.

The G iantShort-facedKangar oo was

two to thr ee metr estall and weig hed

mor e tha n 200 kilograms.

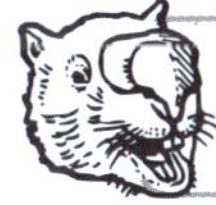

One way to check your spacing is to place a square between words.

Copy the text, then check your spacing. Colour a small square between every word.

The ■ Giant Short-faced Kangaroo is

now extinct. You can see its fossilised

remains in the Naracoorte Caves.

ISBN: 9780170424066

Self-assessment: Spacing

Rewrite the text in the box below in cursive. Remember to use even spacing.

The Victoria Fossil Cave is one of the Naracoorte Caves. It hides many fossils of ancient animals that roamed the area long ago.

Copy the text. Remember to check your spacing.

In 1969, two explorers stumbled across

a narrow gap in Victoria Fossil Cave.

Inside was a huge chamber of fossils.

Self-assessment

Rate the spacing in your handwriting.

It's sometimes even.

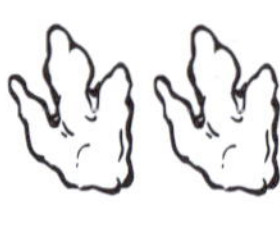

It's mostly even.

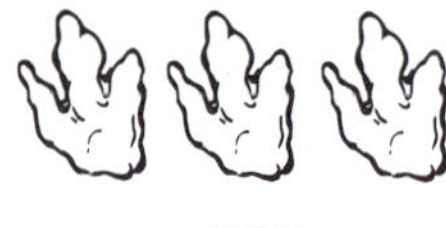

My spacing is always even!

Slope

A consistent slope helps to keep your handwriting legible.

Slope lines can be drawn on the vertical parts of a letter. Using a ruler, continue to mark the slope lines in 'megafauna'.

Now, write 'Naracoorte Caves' in cursive, using the slope lines as a guide.

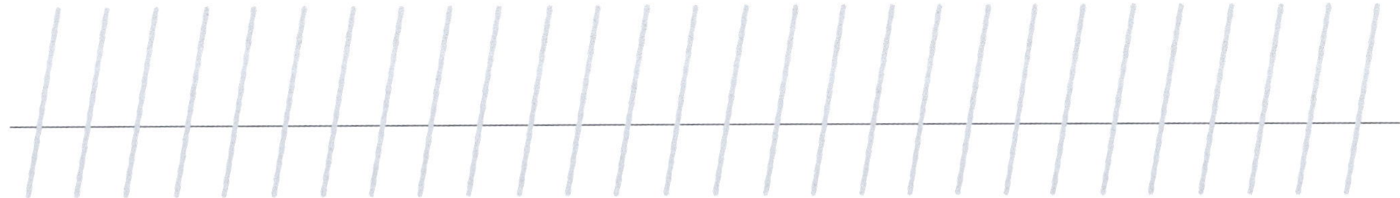

Trace and finish these patterns. Try to keep a consistent slope.

ISBN: 9780170424066

Self-assessment: Slope

Copy these words, then check your slope. Draw slope lines on the vertical parts of the letters.

imprints

species

giant

chamber

bones

discover

Self-assessment

How consistent is the slope of your handwriting?

I need practice.

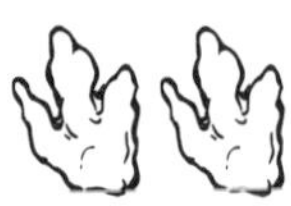

My slope is fairly consistent.

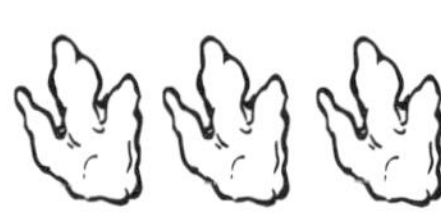

My slope is always consistent!

ISBN: 9780170424066

The letter 'e'

Remember: dip the join a bit lower when joining horizontally from b, o, r, v or w to 'e'.

lower dip

be oe re ve we

Trace and copy.

be oe re ve we be oe re ve we

Thredbo resort believe weather

wellbeing Yarrangobilly Caves event

creature Snowy River awesome

Alpine Way Drive flowers joey rein

ISBN 9780170424066

ce

When joining diagonally to 'e', change the shape of the 'e' slightly. Have the letters join below the magic line.

Trace and copy.

ae de ie le ce he ke pe

Copy.

glacier peak poles sediment valley

highest granite challenge slopes leads

e → erosion

No entry is needed when 'e' is at the start of a word.

Copy.

elevation environment early every

enchanting emerge energy equal

ISBN: 9780170424066

Practise joining horizontally and diagonally to the letter 'e'. Copy the text.

Thredbo is a lovely place to stay in

a ski resort and benefit from exercising

in beautiful, crisp mountain air. Such

wonderful weather is terrific for your

health and wellbeing. The Alpine Way

Drive has remarkable scenery and

you may even spot a wild brumby.

These horses have lived in the Mount

Kosciuszko area for over 200 years.

ISBN: 9780170424066

Rewrite the text in the box below in cursive. Take special care with your joins to 'e'.

Banjo Paterson's poem 'The Man from Snowy River' describes wild brumbies that are born and bred to run free on the mountain slopes. The poem was written in 1890 and is still read today.

Peer review

Ask your partner to give you some feedback on how well you wrote the text above. Ask them to notice how carefully you completed your joins to the letter 'e'.

2 stars (two things you did well)

1 wish (a way for you to improve)

ISBN: 9780170424066

The letter 's'

rs

When joining to 's' from the letters b, o, r or w, make a careful horizontal sweep, then retrace the top part of 's' before completing the letter.

Trace and copy.

bs os rs ws bs os rs ws

Kosciuszko observe cars paws posts

es

Use a diagonal join to join other letters to 's'. Modify the shape of the 's' to speed up your writing.

Trace and copy.

as cs ds es is ks ls ms ns ts

rocks trails skis sleds trees

ascent plains majestic mountains

ISBN: 9780170424066

Remember to speed up your handwriting by joining from the letter 's'. Retrace along the bottom of the letter.

Trace and copy.

sc si sl sn sa si sm

so sq st sy sp sr su

Trace and copy the words, then copy the sentence.

snow summit spectacular saddle

south slight scenery biggest tallest

The summit walk provides hikers with a spectacular view of the snow-capped mountain range.

ISBN: 9780170424066

Practise joining to and from the letter 's'. Copy the text.

Tessa and Lawson felt excited that 4M was having an excursion to Kosciuszko National Park. Their school bus travelled carefully up the ascent. Tessa dreamed about rushing through the snow on skis or a sled, as she looked out at the road ahead. Lawson spotted a majestic waterfall just beyond some rocky trails.

ISBN 9780170424066

Work with a partner to order these mountain peaks from smallest to largest in elevation. Using cursive, write the mountain peaks in height order below. It might be helpful to cross off each one as you order it correctly. Be careful when joining to the letter 's'.

Mount Kosciusko 2228 m
Carruthers Peak 2145 m
Mount Townsend 2209 m
Muellers Peak 2120 m
Rams Head 2190 m
Alice Rawson Peak 2160 m

Peer review

Ask your partner to give you some feedback on how well you wrote the text above. Ask them to notice how carefully you completed your joins to the letter 's'.

2 stars (two things you did well)

1 wish (a way for you to improve)

ISBN: 9780170424066

The letter 'f'

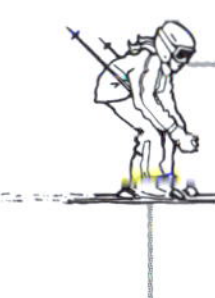

When joining to 'f', the loop crosses at the magic line.

Trace and copy these letter pairs with diagonal joins to 'f', then copy the words below.

if af lf ef uf mf nf df

safety beautiful wildflowers swiftly

lift twelfth comfort bonfire unfold

Trace and copy these letter pairs with horizontal joins to 'f', then copy the text below.

of rf wf of rf wf

soft colourful snowfall powerful

In springtime, the snow slowly melts and colourful wildflowers begin to bloom.

ISBN 9780170424066

Remember: when 'f' is at the beginning of a word, it doesn't need a loop.

Trace and copy.

fun family fantastic flight flicker

fe

Remember to drop down the crossbar to go from 'f' to 'e'.

Trace and copy.

fern feral fear few felt

feet fellow fetch feat fee

fo

Remember to retrace when joining from 'f' to 'o'.

Trace and copy.

forest folklore forgot forever

ISBN: 9780170424066

waterfall

Remember: use a loop when 'f' is in the middle of a word.

Copy.

raft swiftly soft lift safe

Practise joining to and from the letter 'f'. Copy the riddle below.

Q: A carrot, a scarf, a hat and a few pieces of coal were left near the ski lifts. Why were they left there?

A: A child built a snowman. After the soft snow swiftly melted, those few objects were left behind.

ISBN: 9780170424066

Rewrite the text in the box below in cursive. Be careful with your joins to and from 'f'.

Riding a ski lift for the first time can be a challenge. It is important to pull down the safety bar once you are on the lift. After you reach the top, lift the safety bar and ski away swiftly.

Peer review

Ask your partner to give you some feedback on how well you wrote the text above. Ask them to notice how carefully you completed your 'f' joins.

2 **stars** (two things you did well)

1 **wish** (a way for you to improve)

ISBN: 9780170424066

Joining to 'x'

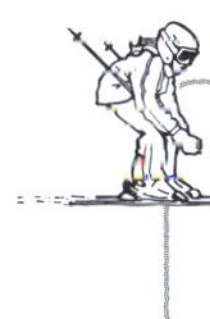

To join to 'x', extend the exit of the previous letter, make a clockwise turn, then lift your pen to form the second stroke of the letter 'x'.

Trace and copy these letter pairs with diagonal joins to 'x'.

ax ex ix ux nx ax ex ix ux nx

Copy.

exist extreme mixed explore relax

luxury exercise fixed anxiety jinx

ox

When joining horizontally from 'o' to 'x', make a slight dip as you sweep across to form the first stroke of 'x'.

Trace and copy.

ox ox ox ox ox ox ox ox

Copy.

fox equinox lunchbox toxic oxygen

ISBN: 9780170424066

Joining to 'z'

To join to 'z', make a diagonal sweep up to the top of the 'z'.

az

Trace these letter pairs with diagonal joins to 'z'.

az ez iz uz az ez iz uz

Copy.

amazing breeze blizzard horizon

When joining from 'o' to 'z', make a smooth horizontal sweep across to the top of the 'z'.

oz

Trace these words with 'oz' joins.

snooze bulldozer frozen ozone dozens

Copy.

A horse ride can be an amazing way

to see the high country. Have a lazy

afternoon snooze, then wake up ready

to see the sky ablaze with sunset colours.

ISBN: 9780170424066

Self-assessment: All tricky joins

Copy the text, paying careful attention to the words with tricky joins.

It is lovely to explore the Snowy Mountains region after the first soft snow falls. If you exit left after Canberra, to historic Cooma, you can learn amazing facts about the Snowy Mountains hydro-electricity scheme, Australia's biggest construction project.

Self-assessment

Rate your tricky joins.

☐ I need more practice.

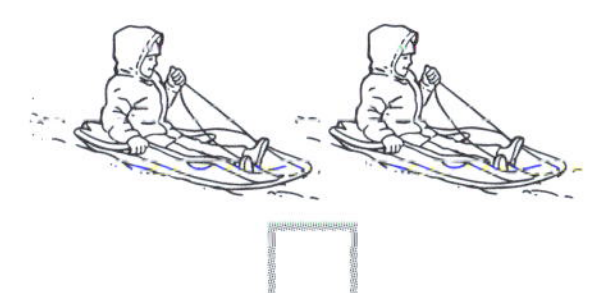

☐ They are getting better.

☐ My tricky joins are excellent!

ISBN: 9780170424066

Correct letter formation

Revise correct letter formation. Copy the text in the box below using unjoined letters.

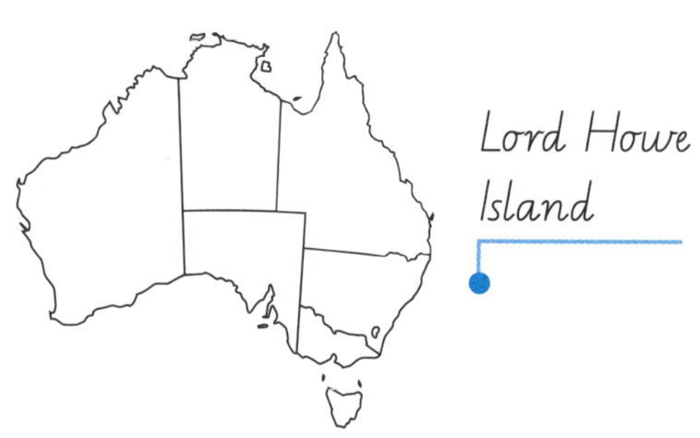

Lord Howe Island is a special place. It belongs to an island group located 700 kilometres north-east of Sydney. It originated as a large shield volcano. Over time, 90% of the volcano has been eroded by the sea, leaving a crescent shaped island.

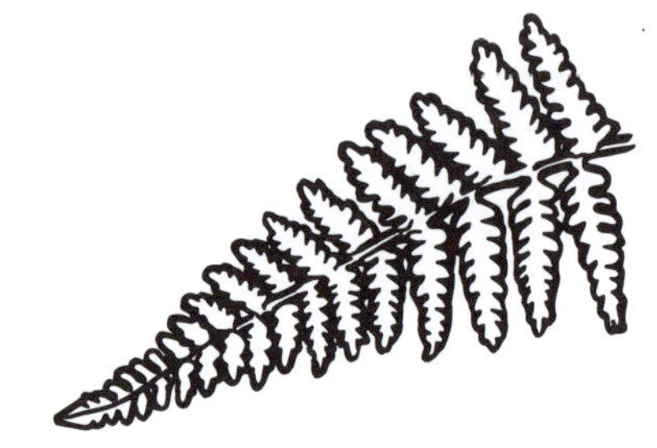

Double letter pairs

Practise double letter pairs with horizontal joins. Trace and copy.

bb oo rr vv bb oo rr vv

pool scooped burrow bubble bloom

oss

Remember: when double 's' comes after a horizontal join, modify the second 's'.

Trace and copy.

possible albatross fossick possess

ff

1 2 3

When writing double 'f', extend the crossbar of the first 'f' upwards to make a loop for the second 'f'.

Trace and copy.

ff ff ff ff ff ff ff

different suffer affirm offend

ISBN: 9780170424066

Practise double letter pairs with diagonal joins. Trace and copy.

cc dd ee ll mm nn pp

tonnes allow feeders swimming

stunned rudder shallow ripple

iss

When double 's' comes after a diagonal join, both letters are modified.

Trace and copy.

pass mess guess hiss miss fuss

amass harmless permission dissolve

ISBN: 9780170424066

Copy the text, paying particular attention to double letter pairs.

A small, flightless insect was discovered on Balls Pyramid, a tall, craggy outcrop off the coast of Lord Howe Island. It was almost allowed to become extinct when rats were introduced to the island.

In 2001, David Priddel and Nicholas Carlile scooped up some eggs. Melbourne Zoo now supports a breeding program.

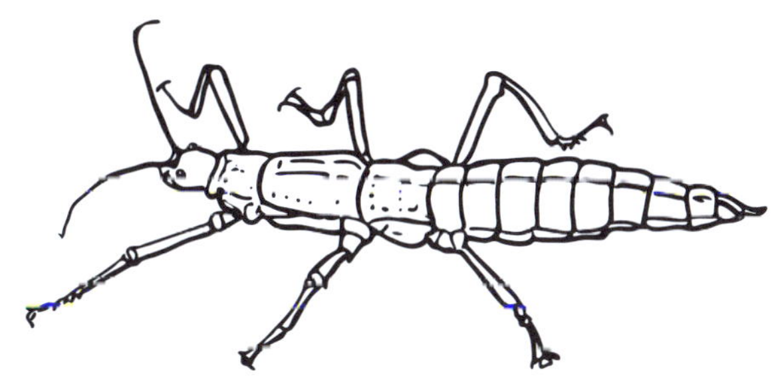

ISBN: 9780170424066

Common letter clusters

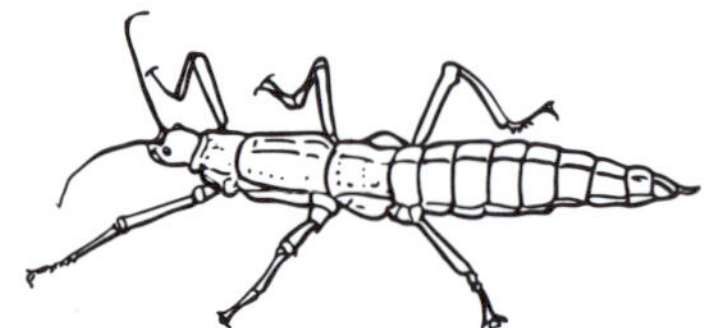

Trace and copy these common letter clusters. Copy the words.

two letter initial consonant blends

bl blisters   br bright   cl clownfish

cr crest   dr drive   gl glisten   fr frozen

sl slip   pr prickle   sc scuba   sk skip

sm small   fl flathead   tr trench

two letter final consonant blends

ft lift   ld fold   lk walk   lt halt

mp ramp   nd sand   ng rang

nt tent   nk ink   rd word   sk ask

py happy   st best   wn lawn

ISBN: 9780170424066

three letter initial consonant blends

scr scream   thr throw   str strap

spl splinter   spr sprinkle   sph sphere

squ squeal   shr shrink   sch school

digraphs

ar car   ou shout   er water   or fork

ch chalk   ee queen   sh ship

th throw   ll small   aw paw

ay play   oa boat   ea sea   ow owl

get.ga/PMWA172

ISBN: 9780170424066

Classifying joins

Copy the text, then complete the activity below.

The Tasmanian Wilderness is one of the last genuine wilderness regions in the world. Many people go hiking in the national parks there. One of the most photographed landmarks is Cradle Mountain.

Find letter pairs in the text above for each join type.

diagonal joins ______

touch joins ______

horizontal joins ______

letters with non-joining descenders ______

joins to ascenders ______

ISBN: 9780170424066

Revising touch joins

If you retrace the top of the anti-clockwise letters a, c, d, g and q, it slows down your handwriting. Touch joins are quicker.

Copy the text with touch joins.

The walking trails in Tasmania cross many rugged, mountainous areas.

Make two rows of letter pairs with touch joins. Then use your letter pairs to make words.

a c e i l u n m to a c d g q

get.gg/PMWA173

Pen lifts

Using pen lifts makes handwriting easier by helping your hand to move easily across the page.

Add a dot to indicate the pen lifts in each word. Don't forget the touch joins.

weather eucalyptus vehicle

bushwalking holiday

wilderness changeable

Tasmania icicle adventure

Prove your answers by writing the words in two colours, changing colour every time you lift your pencil.

Converting between scripts

Complete the table.

Unjoined	Cursive	Capital letters
Tasmania	Tasmania	TASMANIA
	park	
		PLATYPUS
mountain		
	bushwalk	
		LAKE
island		
	beauty	
		WATERFALL
weather		
	tourists	
		FLORA
fauna		
	wombat	
		SPECIES

Circle the script you find most comfortable to write.

unjoined   cursive   CAPITAL LETTERS

ISBN: 9780170424066

Numerals

Read the facts, then copy the numerals and number words below.

- The Tasmanian Wilderness is $\frac{1}{5}$ of the area of the state.
- The Overland Track is 73 km long.
- Tasmania is 240 km south of the Australian mainland.
- Tasmania is the 26th largest island in the world.
- An adult male Tasmanian devil is about 65 cm in length, and weighs up to 12 kg.

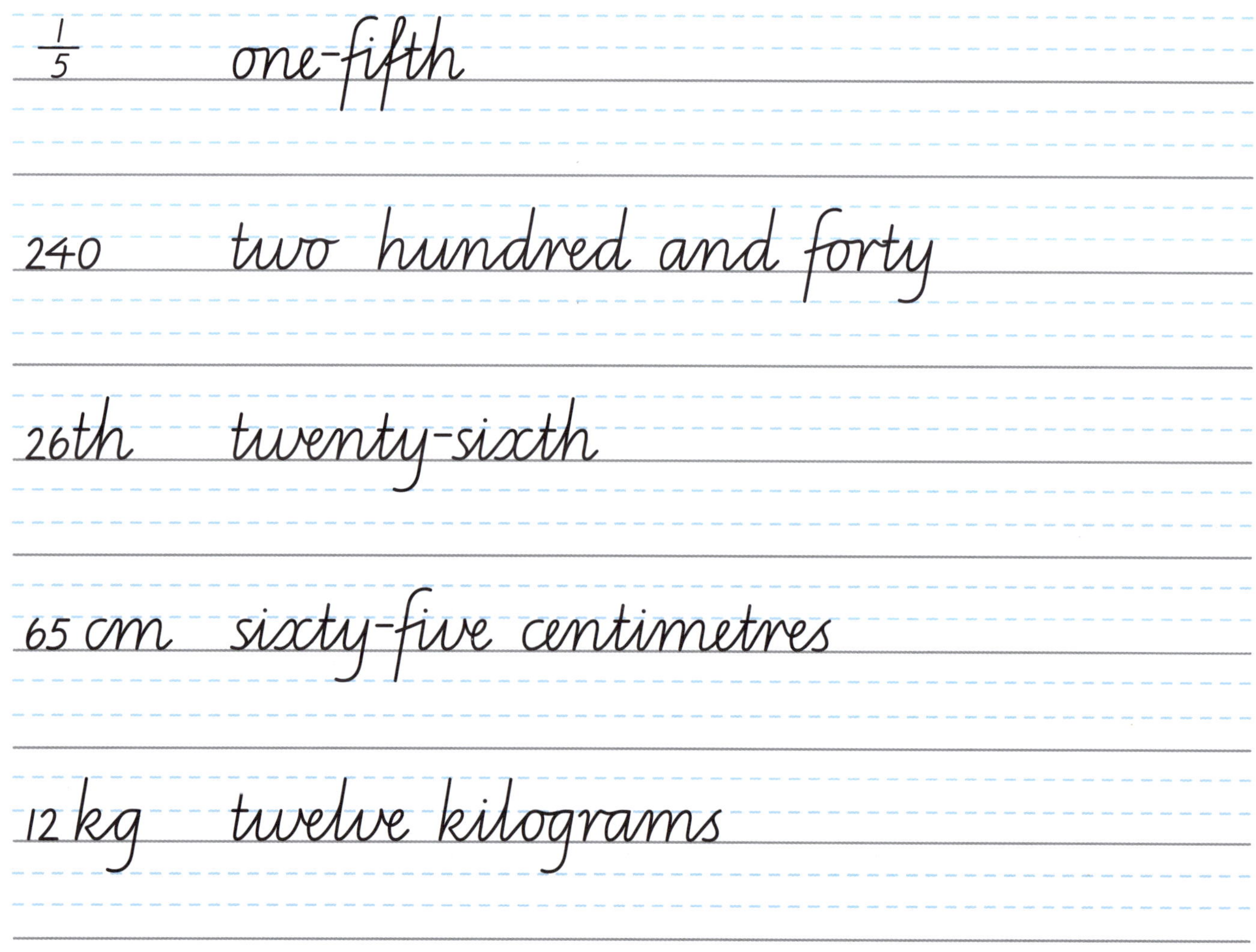

Revising size, spacing and slope

The size, spacing and slope of your handwriting can all affect how legible it is.

Copy these words in the spaces provided. Be careful to keep the size of your letters the same as the models.

get.ga/PMWA174

geography Tasmania hiking mapping

distance mountain fieldwork bushland

climb adventure cold protect track

environment country kinship respect

Sometimes you need to write at different sizes. Can you change the size of your writing and maintain your legibility?

walk walk walk walk

ISBN: 9780170424066

Rewrite the text in the box below in cursive, then check your word spacing. Colour a small square between every word.

Tasmanian devils can be found in the wild in Tasmania. Devils became extinct on the mainland thousands of years ago. They are now endangered in Tasmania, too.

Rewrite the text with correct letter spacing.

A Tasmania n tiger was t he size of
a d og. It had st ripes on its back
an d a pouch, lik e a kan gar oo.

ISBN: 9780170424066

Copy the text, then check your slope. Draw slope lines on the vertical parts of the letters.

Tasmanian devils are black but can

have white fur on their rump or chest.

Practise writing the word 'legible', using the slope lines as a guide.

legible

Now write a word of your own.

Trace and copy these patterns. Try to maintain an even slope.

fff lll elele

Speed loops to letters with ascenders

Speed loops can make your handwriting more fluent. You have less to retrace.

coral → coral

When using a speed loop to join to b, h, k or l, make sure the loop and the ascender meet at the magic line.

Trace and copy these letter pairs with speed loops to ascenders.

al mb ub ch sh th ck rk sk al ll

Copy these words with speed loops to ascenders.

shore snorkelling bubble climb

Copy the text.

Ningaloo Reef is rich in colourful coral,

tropical fish, turtles and whale sharks.

Speed loops from letters with descenders

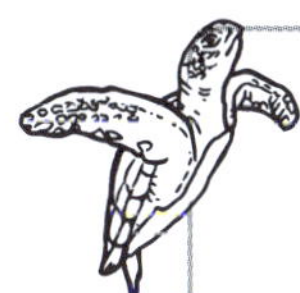

When making a speed loop from g, j, y or z, trail your pen from the end of the letter, crossing at the baseline.

Ningaloo

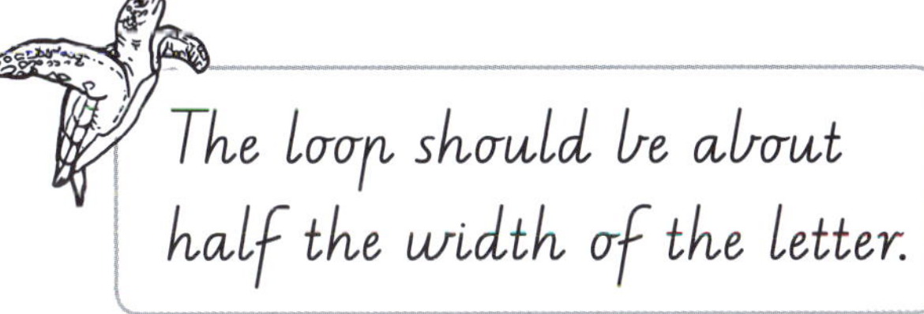

get.ga/PMWA175

Trace and copy these letter pairs with speed loops from descenders.

ga gl gr ja ju je ye yi yo za zi zo

Copy these words with speed loops from descenders.

dugongs rejoice rays playful ozone

delight flight eagle puzzle sizzling

Copy the text.

Angie was delighted to see a group of playful dugongs when visiting Ningaloo.

ISBN: 9780170424066

When to avoid speed loops

snorkelling

A speed loop is not needed if g, j, y or z is at the end of a word.

Copy these words.

swimming along display enjoy blitz

habitat

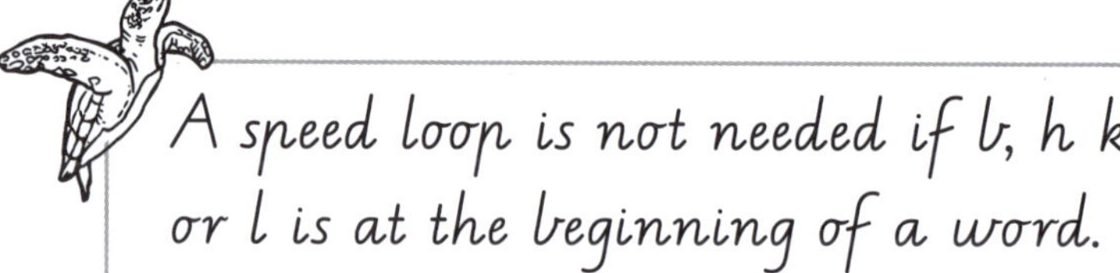

Copy these words.

heritage harmless beach kayak leaf

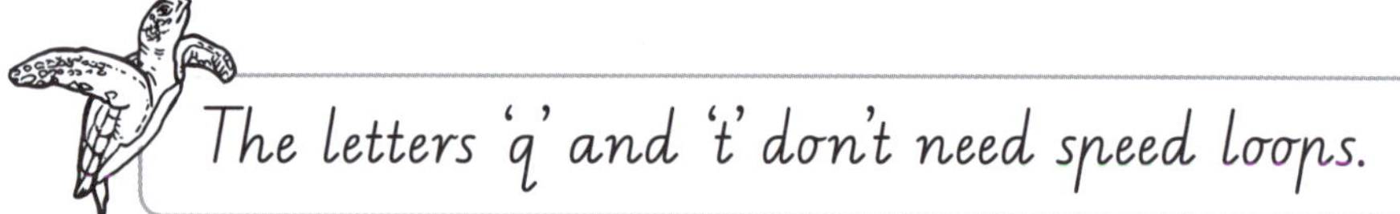

Rewrite the text in cursive, using speed loops where they are needed.

There are many ways to enjoy Coral
Bay – paddle a kayak, go kitesurfing
or quietly watch humpback whales.

Practising speed loops

Copy the text, paying careful attention to your speed loops.

Ningaloo Reef is a breeding ground for green and loggerhead turtles. The loggerhead turtle is the most endangered type of turtle in the world. It got its name from its large head, which looks like a big log. Loggerheads migrate huge distances to their nesting grounds. A female might travel 12000 kilometres to get back to the beach where she was a baby.

Rewrite the text in the box below in your best cursive handwriting. Remember to use speed loops correctly.

My visit to the reef was fascinating! As soon as I put my mask on the surface of the water, I had an incredible view of this marine environment. The purple and pink colours of the coral were quite striking. My sister, Isla, saw a school of clownfish. There were several of them swimming along together.

get.ga/PMWA176

Mapping a journey around Australia

Label the states and territories of Australia on the map. Use all capital letters.

QUEENSLAND	VICTORIA	NORTHERN TERRITORY
NEW SOUTH WALES	SOUTH AUSTRALIA	AUSTRALIAN CAPITAL TERRITORY
TASMANIA	WESTERN AUSTRALIA	

Turn the page sideways to draw the Aboriginal flag in the box and then use the correct colours to colour it in.

Final self-assessment

Copy the text.

The Whale Shark is the largest fish in the sea. It is as large as many whales but it is a fish, not a mammal. The mouth of a Whale Shark can be up to 1.5 metres wide and can contain 300 rows of tiny teeth. Even though it is a fish, it is a filter feeder like many whales.

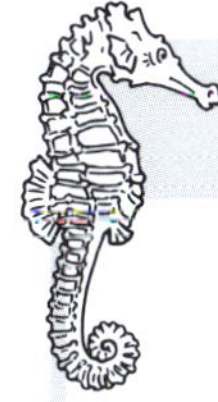

Self-assessment

Rate your Victorian Modern Cursive script.

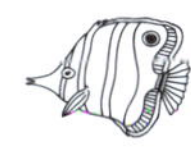

☐ It's getting there.

☐ It's good.

☐ My cursive handwriting is excellent!

Teacher observation guide

Student is: left-handed ☐ right-handed ☐

Student demonstrates correct posture, paper position and pencil grip. ☐

Student uses smaller writing lines with accuracy. ☐

Student forms Victorian Modern Cursive (lower-case and capital letters) with accuracy. ☐

Student forms numerals with accuracy. ☐

Student forms the following joins with accuracy:

- diagonal joins ☐
- touch joins ☐
- horizontal joins ☐
- tricky joins to and from the letters e, s, f, x and z ☐
- joins using speed loops ☐

Student can identify the letters that do not join in Victorian Modern Cursive. ☐

Student can convert between scripts: unjoined, cursive and capital letters. ☐

Student can copy a complete passage of text with accuracy using Victorian Modern Cursive. ☐

Student can identify when a pen lift is required. ☐

Student has an understanding of factors that influence legibility (size, spacing, slope). ☐

Student can self-assess with accuracy. ☐

Notes:

....

....

Date:

....

CERTIFICATE

get.ga/PMWC170